JAN POLKOWSKI

GŁOSY / VOICES

  Ministry of **Culture** National Heritage and **Sport** of the Republic of **Poland.**

GŁOSY / VOICES

by Jan Polkowski

Translated from the Polish by Charles S. Kraszewski

with an afterword by Józef Maria Ruszar

Edited by Aeddan Shaw and Magdalena Filipczuk

Cover photo 'Stocznia Gdańska. Zamknięte' by Maria Gąsecka

Publishers Maxim Hodak & Max Mendor

© 2021, Jan Polkowski

© 2021, Charles S. Kraszewski

Afterword © 2021, Józef Maria Ruszar

Photographs © 2021, Maria Gąsecka

© 2021, Glagoslav Publications

www.glagoslav.com

ISBN: 978-1-914337-34-5
ISBN: 978-83-66765-78-8

First published in English by Glagoslav Publications in October 2021

A catalogue record for this book is available from the British Library.

This book is in copyright. No part of this publication may be reproduced, stored in a retrieval system or transmitted in any form or by any means without the prior permission in writing of the publisher, nor be otherwise circulated in any form of binding or cover other than that in which it is published without a similar condition, including this condition, being imposed on the subsequent purchaser.

JAN POLKOWSKI

GŁOSY / VOICES

Translated from the Polish by Charles S. Kraszewski
with an afterword by Józef Maria Ruszar

GLAGOSLAV PUBLICATIONS

TREŚĆ

Szkwał. W zimnej koszuli idę wzdłuż zatoki	8
Wierzę, że nie masz do mnie żalu. Oprócz ciebie miałam	14
Przeźroczystymi rękami robiłaś mi kanapki	18
Lubię zatłoczony kościół, nie widzę wtedy nikogo	20
Krótki ruch powietrza po twoim niedbałym geście	22
Kochany Tato, strasznie Cię nienawidziłem	26
Nie powiedziałam ci, że jestem w ciąży	28
Opłatek, Wigilia, mama w popielatej sukni	30
Wolność. Myślałem o niej kiedy ciepłą nocą	34
Patrzę na moje paznokcie — nierówno pomalowane	36
Składam się z niepamięci od paznokci po nerki	38
Nie wiem jak to jest być sierotą. Mama, siostra	40
Zawieźli mnie na cmentarz, chcieli zakopać ciało.	42
Kim miałem zostać? Nikim. Bo czy miałem przeżyć?	46
Sam nie wiem właściwie dlaczego	48
Słońce jeszcze nie wstało, leży na mokrym piasku	50
Mieszkając w tobie myślę czasem czy rozumiałeś	52
Senność, senność, senność, fale kroków gasnące	54
Czy poezja nie powinna być szczególnie wyczulona...	58

CONTENTS

Squall. In a cold shirt I walk along the bay 9
I know that you don't blame me. Besides you, I had 15
With transparent hands you made me sandwiches 19
I like a crowded church for then I can see no one 21
The short shift of air following your casual gesture 23
Dearest Daddy how sincerely I hated you 27
I didn't tell you I was pregnant 29
The Christmas Eve opłatek mama in her ashen dress 31
Freedom. I thought of it on each warm night 35
I look at my nails — unevenly painted 37
I'm made up of oblivion from nails to kidneys 39
I don't know what it's like to be an orphan. Mother, sister . 41
They took me to the graveyard they wanted to bury the body . . 43
Who was I supposed to become? No one.
Because was I supposed to survive at all? 47
I myself don't know why 49
The sun's not yet arisen it lies on the wet sand 51
Living in you I wonder sometimes have you come to understand . 53
Sleepiness sleepiness sleepiness the dying waves of steps . . 55
Should poetry not be particularly sensitive to unspoken… . . 59

'Jan Polkowski's *Voices* — The Antigones of the Baltic Coast'
by Józef Maria Ruszar 61
Bibliography 85
About the author 87
List of works by Jan Polkowski 89
About the translator 91
List of photographs by Maria Gąsecka 92
About the photographer 93

GŁOSY / VOICES

* * *

Szkwał. W zimnej koszuli idę wzdłuż zatoki.
Kim byłem? Ziarenkiem piasku pod stopą rybitwy
kapitanem fregaty w czapce po stryju Władku
sercem szybkich jaskółek z kratkowanego papieru
specem od gry w nożyka i Wyścig Pokoju
wiecznym utrapieniem mojej biednej mamy
bo zamiast ministrantury wolałem mecze w nogę.
Trudno wyliczyć wszystkie magiczne wcielenia.
Zasypiając czułem jak przy skroni wiruje poduszka
Ziemi a w głowie tną kosmos milknące
gwiazdy. Życie. Szesnaście ogromnych lat.
Przebiegały tak lekko, że zapominałem oddychać
a kiedy ochłonąłem przyszedł dzień odczytania.

W tym dniu moje życie trwało tylko godzinę.
O czwartej trzydzieści obudziłem się w bloku.
A do piątej czterdzieści otwierał się los.
Poznałem ludzką podłość, pragnienia
i tajemnice czystej, mądrej wolności.
Burzliwą przyjaźń z Żeromskim zakończyłem kłótnią.
Przed kolegami ukryłem jak zabrzmiało we mnie
przekleństwo zdania Norwida *Czemu cieniu odjeżdżasz…*
Ściągnąłem od Leonarda schemat lekkich skrzydeł.
Nie uciekłem daleko. Zostałem niewolnikiem
lunatycznych spacerów z Dorotą córką spawacza
ze Stoczni Marynarki Wojennej i Afrodyty Zimnych Mórz
uwięzionej w bezkształtnej sukience z bistoru.
Tak, zostałem ojcem, czy dobrym doprawdy nie wiem.

* * *

Squall. In a cold shirt I walk along the bay.
Who was I? A grain of sand beneath a tern's foot
a frigate captain wearing Uncle Władek's cap
the heart of swift swallows made of notepad paper
an expert in mumbly-peg and the Race of Peace
the eternal thorn in my poor mother's side
who preferred soccer match to Sunday Mass.
It's hard to sum up all the magical incarnations.
Falling asleep I felt beneath my temple
the pillow of the world spin, stars
fading away slicing through the cosmos in my head.
Life. Sixteen immense years.
They passed so softly I forgot to breathe
and when I cooled down came the day of reckoning.

On that day my life lasted one hour only.
At four thirty I woke up in the flat
and destiny was open till five forty.
I came to know the human villainy of desire
and the secrets of pure wise freedom.
My stormy friendship with Żeromski ended in a quarrel.
Before my friends I hid the inner swelling
of Norwid's cursing words *O Shade why art thou departing…*
From Leonardo I copied a diagram of filmy wings.
I didn't get far. I became enslaved
to moonlight walks with Dorota the daughter
of a welder from the Military Shipyards
and Aphrodite of the Cold Seas
imprisoned in a shapeless crimplene dress.
And so I became a father a good one? I really don't know.

Dzieci nie pamiętam lub boję się wspomnieć
ich lniane zadziorne stópki i słowa jak skóra świata.
Uczyłem się starości. Bóg pojawiał się, znikał.
Z wysokich słów schodził Chrystus bym wątpił
i dotykał. Podróże? Do Krakowa i na rowerze
za miasto przez nieprzebyty gąszcz słodkich sierpniowych obietnic.
Tym razem żyłem uważnie hamując obroty Ziemi
by czuć jak stygną w zmierzchu piaszczyste ścieżki czasu.

Pocisk przedzierał się długo przez szron i stukot szyn
przez ranne zgniecione światła wymieszane z olejem
zabłoconego słońca by wreszcie przebić mi szyję
przez okno trójmiejskiej kolejki.
Cóż, musicie uwierzyć, że wszystko przeżyłem w godzinę
bo przecież nie zmartwychwstałem a wciąż mam szesnaście lat.
Jeśli kłamię i nie spotkało mnie co spotkać przecież musiało
to wierzcie — świat żaden
naprawdę nigdy
nie istniał.

Zastrzelony? (1954-1970?)

I don't remember my children or maybe I'm afraid to
recall their feisty flaxen feet their words like the world's rind.
I learned old age. God appeared vanished.
And Christ came down from high words so I might doubt
and touch. Trips? To Kraków and on bicycle
beyond the city through the dense thickets of sweet
August promises.
This time I was living carefully brake-pedalling the earth's rotations
to feel how they cool down in the dust, the sandy paths of time.

The bullet took a long time splitting the frost the rattle of rails
the crushed light of morning
mixed with the oil of the muddied sun
until it finally pierced my neck
through the window of the Tricity tram.
Well then you must believe it I lived through it all
in that one hour
for I haven't resurrected after all
I'm still always sixteen.
If I'm lying and none of this happened to me
as it must have happened really
believe this then — no world
ever really existed
ever.

Shot dead? (1954-1970?)

* * *

Wierzę, że nie masz do mnie żalu. Oprócz ciebie miałam
jeszcze trójkę. Trochę zdziwionego swoim istnieniem
Adasia, Józia sprytnego jak dotąd nikt w naszej rodzinie
i Asię, małomówny dowód na istnienie dobra.
Ojciec zgasł szybko i odtąd po zmroku nie mogłam
pozbierać myśli. Praca, kolejki, gotowanie, przerabianie
ubrań. Z dorosłych na dzieci ze starszych na młodsze.
Wydawało mi się, że nigdy nie zasnę, że tylko zastygam
z żelazkiem, igłą i naparstkiem, ciastem na makaron
przygnieciona odłamkiem serca. Chciałam umrzeć
ze wstydu, że żyję. Z nieustępliwej miłości i ze strachu
przed twoim rozrzuconym bezładnie cieniem. Teraz dobijam
osiemdziesiątki więc czas byś mi przebaczył. To ja
wykarmiłam własnym ciałem te bezkresne szeregi bezradnych
dni. I wiem, każdy z nich zabijał cię jeszcze raz
synku.

Matka? (1928-2009?)

* * *

I know that you don't blame me. Besides you, I had
three others. Adaś somewhat stunned at his own existence
Józio clever as no one yet in all our family
and Asia who spoke little — proof that goodness exists.
Your father expired quickly and since then I've had trouble
gathering my thoughts in the darkness. Work queues cooking altering
clothes. From adults to children from older to younger.
It seemed that I would never fall asleep just grow cold
needle in hand thimble on finger macaroni dough
pressed flat by a shard of my heart. I wanted to die
from shame that I'm alive. From implacable love from fear
of your sprawled shadow. Now I'm nearing
eighty so I guess it's high time for you to forgive me. It was me
who fed with my own body that endless range of helpless
days. And I know that each one of them killed you over and over again
my son.

Mother? (1928-2009?)

* * *

Przeźroczystymi rękami robiłaś mi kanapki.
Wbijałaś po omacku nóż w nieruchome morze.
Robiłaś mi kanapki, kroiłaś kulę ziemską
na równe, schludne kromki. Do chlebaka
z brezentu chowałaś godziny rozłąki.
Do szarego papieru wkładałaś dziecięce twarze.
Gładziłaś mnie po policzku jakbym miał iść na wojnę
jakby drzwi były z ognia a nie z płyty pilśniowej.
Wchodziłem potem ostrożnie do szatni elektryków
i odwijałem papier by patrzeć jak wolno
znikasz.

Zastrzelony? (1948-1970?)

* * *

With transparent hands you made me sandwiches.
Blindly, you plunged your knife into the quiet sea.
You made me sandwiches you sliced the earthly globe
into neat even pieces. You stuffed my canvas
knapsack with hours of farewell.
You wrapped the children's faces in grey paper.
You stroked my cheek as if I were going off to war
as if the door was made of fire and not of fibreboard.
Later, I made my careful way into the electricians' lockers
and unfolded the paper to watch you slowly disappearing.

Shot dead? (1948 – 1970?)

* * *

Lubię zatłoczony kościół, nie widzę wtedy nikogo.
Chowam się przed Bogiem. Nie chcę widzieć siebie.
Lituję się bardziej nad Nim niż nad samą sobą.
Śmierci się nie boję jeśli należy do mnie.
Lubię iść w ciemności, wzdłuż omdlałego morza
wyławiać z wiatru wspomnienia
tulić ich stopy jak piasek tuli spokojny brzeg.
Dziwić się nowym szczegółom:
gdy nosiłam cię w sobie niecierpliwie, ze złością
a ty kopałeś mnie mocno i pchałeś ku przyszłości.
Milczący. Taki jak dzisiaj.

Matka? (1931-?)

* * *

I like a crowded church for then I can see no one.
Although I hide from God I don't want to see me either.
I feel sorrier for Him than for myself.
I'm not afraid of death if it's my death.
I like to stroll in the darkness along the fainting sea
snatching memories from the wind
cradling their feet as the sand cradles the calm shore.
To wonder at new details:
like how I carried you about inside me impatiently angrily
and you would kick me hard pushing me toward the future.
Silently. Just like today.

Mother? (1931-?)

* * *

Krótki ruch powietrza po twoim niedbałym geście
dryfuje w mojej głowie. Sunie rozlaną Wisłą
wypływa w żywe morze. Widzę już tylko ciebie
i bezmiar szepcącej wody. Co miałbym widzieć? Ty jesteś
moim synem, ja całe życie bełtałem los na pokładach statków.
Cóż więc innego mam widzieć jeśli nie kołyszącą światem
połyskującą falę, rybią łuskę śmierci
krę krwawiącego brzegu. Teraz moim morzem
jest kuchenny stół a z pokładu zmywa mnie jak śmieci
bezbrzeżna noc. Żona śpi, ciebie nie ma
nawet w tętnie śniegu. Więc płynę samotnie
ku rozmytym światłom dzieciństwa.
Czy spotkam cię po drodze? I choćby na chwilę
przysiądziemy na piasku? Będziemy
razem młodnieć? Jak boje uderzać z wiatrem
w fale leniwej przyszłości skulonej w tobie
na dnie?

Ojciec? (1924-2003?)

* * *

The short shift of air following your casual gesture
drifts in my head. Slips on the spreading Wisła
out into the living sea. I see only you now
and the immensity of the whispering water. What should I see? You are
my son all my life long I rolled the dice of fate on ship decks.
So what else should I see but the world-rocking
fish-scale of death shimmering on the waves the floe
of the bleeding shore. Now my sea is
the kitchen table like rubbish I'm washed from the deck
by the limitless night. My wife is sleeping you are not
even to be found in the pulse of the snow. So I sail backwards
toward the blurry lights of childhood
will I meet you along the way? And at least for a while
sit down with you on the sand? Will we
grow young together? As buoys struck by the wind
in the waves of the lazy future curled up in you
in the depths?

Father? (1924-2003?)

* * *

Kochany Tato, strasznie Cię nienawidziłem
Dlatego, że Cię nie było a była reszta świata.
Pewnie także dlatego, że dopiekała bieda.
Pomagał nam wujek, parafia, sąsiedzi.
Gdy podrosłem zbierałem butelki, szmaty i złom.
Jedliśmy wodziankę, zacierki, ziemniaki
ziemniaki, ziemniaki. Nienawidziłem Ciebie
bo byłeś gdzie indziej i nie troszczyłeś się o nas.
Kiedy nienawiść stygła patrzyłem na mamę
która gdy nie płakała, płakała jeszcze bardziej.
Wtedy wracała nienawiść i łatwiej było przetrwać.
Myślałem, że zginąłeś dlatego, że nie chciałeś
ciągnąć wielkich ciężarów pod prąd
wielkich słów i by się od nich uwolnić
dałeś trafić się w serce.
Ale może nie byłeś po prostu zwykłym tchórzem?
Polska. Nie umiem o niej mówić.
Widziałem ją w suchych oczach siostrzyczki
i w plecach mamy wstrząsanych nagłym
zakrętem przyszłości. W grudniu rzuciłem wszystko
drukowałem bibułę i siedziałem trochę.
Teraz jestem dekarzem
buduję ludziom dachy.
Od dobrych kilku lat chociaż nie za często
chodzę do Ciebie na cmentarz.

Syn? (1960-?)

* * *

Dearest Daddy how sincerely I hated you
for you went away and the rest of the world stayed right where it was.
For that, and probably too for the sting of poverty that followed.
We were helped out by uncle parish neighbours.
When I was old enough I picked bottles rags and scrap metal.
We ate stale bread soup hasty pudding potatoes
potatoes potatoes I hated you
because you were somewhere else and didn't give a fig for us.
When my hatred cooled I would glance at mama
who when she wasn't sobbing was sobbing all the more.
Then the hatred came back making it easier to muddle through.
I thought you perished because you didn't want
to drag such heavy loads up against the current
of grand words and so to be free of them
you let them shoot you through the heart.
But maybe you were more than a mere coward?
Poland. I don't know how to speak of her.
I saw her in the closed eyes of my little sister
and when mama's back suddenly convulsed
at the sharp turn of the future. In December I threw it all to hell
mimeographed underground stuff sat in gaol a bit.
Now I'm a roofer.
I make roofs for people.
For a few good years now although not too often
I visit you in the graveyard.

Son? (1960-?)

* * *

Nie powiedziałam ci, że jestem w ciąży.
Jesteście tacy podobni, uparci i porywczy
i obaj nie żyjecie, ty i twój syn.
Powtarzam w myśli słowa: Ojcze nasz
Zdrowaś Mario i Wieczne odpoczywanie
z nadzieją, że kiedyś znowu staną się modlitwą
a ja się nią owinę jak swetrem babci Stasi.
Masz takie słabe ręce jak mysie ślady na śniegu
choć jesteś brygadzistą i budujesz statki.
Masz takie niezgrabne stopy i rozchlapujesz Bałtyk
choć jeszcze pijesz ze mnie przez wiotką pępowinę.
Masz takie lekkie usta jakbyś chciał opowiedzieć
synowi co już się nie zdarzy.
Masz takie matowe oczy jakbyś chciał ojca zabrać
do nieba mojego brzucha.

Narzeczona? (1952-?)

* * *

I didn't tell you I was pregnant.
You are so similar both stubborn and impulsive
both unalive you and your son.
In my thoughts I keep repeating words: Our Father
Hail Mary and Eternal rest grant unto them
in hopes that one day they will become a prayer
in which I can wrap myself up like in Grandma Stasia's sweater.
You have such weak hands like mouse tracks on the snow
although you're a foreman building ships.
You have such clumsy feet and you swill your Bałtyk vodka
though you're still drinking from me through your limp umbilical cord
you have such light little lips as if you wanted to tell
your son about everything that now will never happen.
You have such opaque eyes as if you wanted to take your father
into the heaven of my womb.

Fiancée? (1952-?)

* * *

Opłatek, Wigilia, mama w popielatej sukni
kładzie jak każe zwyczaj dodatkowy talerz
przy pustym krześle. Patrzy nieruchomo
przez nas i drżące powietrze, barszcz, rybę
i siano, gałęzie jodły, przez ściany spowite mrozem
na drogę z białego kamienia i pochyloną postać
upadającą pod ciężarem nieuniknionej zdrady.

Brat? (1958-?)

* * *

The Christmas Eve opłatek mama in her ashen dress
sets down as custom dictates a spare plate
by the empty chair. Motionless she stares
right through us and the trembling air the barszcz the fish
the straw the fir branches right through the frost-covered walls
to the street of white stone and the bent figure
falling beneath the weight of inexorable treachery.

Brother? (1958-?)

* * *

Wolność. Myślałem o niej kiedy ciepłą nocą
wchodziłem w labirynt morza. I kiedy z kolegami
wodowałem statek. Albo jak szedłem wieczorem
w poświacie telewizorów samotny jak suche drzewo
wśród pól leżących w gorączce.
Byłem wolny? Bałem się nieustannie, że ktoś
podejdzie cicho i nagle uderzy w głowę.
I zdarzyło się w końcu, dostałem kulę w plecy.
Zdążyłem się odwrócić, widziałem zieleń hełmu
Rude, dziecinne piegi i zdziwione spojrzenie
obejmujące wszystko i nie mające
końca.

Zastrzelony? (1950-1970?)

* * *

Freedom. I thought of it on each warm night
I swam in the labyrinth of the sea or when with chums
we launched a ship. Or when walking at evening
in the half-light of televisions lonely as an arid tree
amidst fields prostrate in the swelter.
Was I free? I was constantly afraid lest someone
come up from behind me quietly and thwack me on the head.
And at last it happened a bullet in the back.
I had time enough to turn around I saw the green of a helmet
red childish freckles and eyes wide open in surprise
taking in everything without
end.

Shot dead? (1950-1970?)

* * *

Patrzę na moje paznokcie — nierówno pomalowane.
Maluję je codziennie, zmywam i znowu maluję.
Maluję, zmywam, maluję.
Poranna msza i paznokcie trzymają mnie w jednym
kawałku. Więc mogę chodzić na cmentarz
do mojego syneczka.
Siostrzenica mi mówi *wiem, że zabili ci syna.*
Skończyło się i trwa tylko w twojej biednej głowie.
Wiem drażni cię ten generał w glorii bohatera
ale pluń na niego.
A ja niczego nie mogę zgasić, zamknąć, zadeptać.
Duchy przychodzą nocą by skamleć i szydzić
w ciszy lśniącej wokół fałszywym, lepkim cieniem.
Mojego ojca wciąż wiozą wagonem towarowym
ku szarym tabunom stepów.
Ja tym samym pociągiem zaryglowanym od zewnątrz
wracam z domu do Polski.
Wiozę w torebce po mące
dwie garście rodzinnej ziemi.

Matka? (1929-?)

* * *

I look at my nails —
unevenly painted.
I paint them every day wipe the polish off paint them again.
Paint wipe paint.
Morning Mass and my fingernails alone keep me in one
piece. And thus I am able to visit my son's
grave. My niece says: *I know they killed your son.*
It's over now it only keeps on happening in your poor head.
I know that general gets under your skin in that aureole of glory
he wears but just spit on him.
But I can't snuff out close out trample down anything.
The ghosts come round at night to yelp and mock
in the silence shining like a false mangled shadow.
They're constantly transporting my father in a cattle car
toward the grey hordes of the steppes.
And I'm constantly in that same wagon bolted from the outside
returning from my home to Poland.
With two handfuls of my native soil
in an old bag of flour.

Mother? (1929-?)

* * *

Składam się z niepamięci od paznokci po nerki
od wątroby po włosy nie pamiętam kim jestem.
Mój sen nie wie kim byłam, mój strach nie wie, że będę.
Jak się mówi przebaczam nie wiem bardziej niż kat.
Jestem sową i wężem choć bardziej nie jestem
niż jestem. Oddycham tylko przyszłością.
Czekam aż fala uderzy, przemyje wędrowny piasek
Dobro, zło i płomyki schylonych za domem trzcin.
Aż spadnie ciężki wiatr. Na skwir sosen
mech zmierzchu.

Matka? (1930-?)

* * *

I'm made up of oblivion from nails to kidneys
from liver to head I can't remember who I am.
My dreams don't know who I was my fear doesn't know that I will be.
How do you say I forgive I don't know any better than the hangman does.
I am owl and snake although I'm more nothing
than anything. I breathe only the future.
Waiting for the falling wave to clean the wandering sand
good evil and the phlox bending over the house of reeds.
For the heavy wind to fall. For the screech of the pines
the moss of nightfall.

Mother? (1930-?)

* * *

Nie wiem jak to jest być sierotą. Mama, siostra
dwóch braci — miałem czternaście lat
kiedy stałem się ojcem dla rodziny i siebie.
Morze uderza w bieguny. Słońce rośnie w źródłach.
Ludzie z nawilgłej soli biegną nieporuszeni.
Ogień ich ściga w zaułkach, zamyka gorące usta.
Stoję nad zgniłą wodą, na brudnym portowym
nabrzeżu. Nigdy i nikomu
już nie dam się przewrócić.

Syn? (1957-?)

* * *

I don't know what it's like to be an orphan. Mother, sister
two brothers — I was fourteen
when I became my family's father and my own.
The sea hammers the poles. The sun grows in the springs.
People of moist salt run on unshakable.
Fire chases them into alleys closes cold lips.
I stand over the putrid water at the dirty port's
shoreline. Never again no one
will I ever allow to push me over.

Son? (1957-?)

* * *

Zawieźli mnie na cmentarz, chcieli zakopać ciało.
Odtąd każdej nocy trwa ten sam obrządek. Wyglądał
jakby zszyli go z jakichś obcych kawałków. Szybko
zamknęli wieko. Wiatr przywlókł znad morza
deszcz i uwiązł w sieci pociemniałych jesionów.
Słychać było jak krople uderzają w sztychówki
i sztychówki jak tłuką ze zgrzytem w kamienie.
Ktoś inny odszedł od studni w ciele Samarytanki.
Ja zostałam. Jak woda. Niema jak pusty
dzban.

Żona? (1950-?)

* * *

They took me to the graveyard they wanted to bury the body.
And from that time on each night the same ritual. He looked
as if they'd sewn him together from unmatching parts. Quick
quick they closed the lid. The wind dragged in the rain
from the sea and got tangled in the net of darkened ash trees.
You could hear the drops battering the spades
the spades battering the ground screeching against the rocks.
Someone else walked away from the well in the Samaritan woman's flesh.
I remained. Like water. Dumb as an empty
jar.

Wife? (1950-?)

* * *

Kim miałem zostać? Nikim. Bo czy miałem przeżyć?
Niewydolność trawienia i nazbyt płytki oddech.
Byłem wcześniakiem w dodatku poród był ciężki okrutnie.
Byłem więc oczkiem w głowie mojej i Boskiej Matki.
Przeżyłem i słabość zmieniła się w pragnienie
buntu przeciwko tępym uderzeniom losu.
To moja krew wypiła biel na fladze
niesionej przez Świętojańską.
Pragnąłem by była czerwonym wiatrem
który zasklepia rany.
Pragnąłem by uderzył z nieuleczalną siłą
w tych, którzy żyć muszą żeby życie ocalić.
Pragnąłem by na zawsze zapisał słowa
tych którzy śmierć przeżyli
jak przed świtem pobudkę i zimną nagość światła
na smukłej stali żurawi i krótkiej rdzawej fali
jak szczęście zanurzone po brzegi
w czasie co cały się spełnił.

Zastrzelony? (1952-1970?)

* * *

Who was I supposed to become? No one. Because was I supposed to
                                                                survive at all?
Inefficient digestion and shortness of breath.
I was a premature child and what's more the delivery was cruel.
And so I became the apple of their eye — mama's and the Virgin Mother's.
I survived and my weakness was transformed into a desire
to revolt against the dull wallops of fate.
It was my blood drunk by the white field of the flag
carried along Świętojańska.
I wanted it to be a red wind
that scabs over wounds.
I wanted it to strike with incurable force
those who must live so as to preserve life.
I wanted it to inscribe forever the words
of those who survived death
such as the reveille before dawn and the cold nakedness of the light
on the slender steel of the crane and the short rusty wave
such as happiness submerged
at a time completely accomplished.

Shot dead? (1952-1970?)

* * *

Sam nie wiem właściwie dlaczego
już nie potrafię zgiąć karku.
Pewnie nie tylko dlatego, że mimo trzech operacji
już zgiąć się po prostu go nie da.
Pewnie nie dlatego, że zginał go zbyt często
mój stary z byle powodu i zawsze by nas chronić.
Cóż, ja jestem kaleką, jego zgnoili przypadkiem.
Matka nie wytrzymała, nie chciała z nim dłużej być.
On szuka teraz uparcie jakiejś chwili lub słowa
o które mógłby zaczepić kolejny dzień
swego życia. Jest już zupełnym staruszkiem.
Myślę, że w sobotę wpadnę do niego
na krótko.

Ranny? (1953-?)

* * *

I myself don't know why
I can't bow my head anymore.
Certainly not just because despite those three operations
It simply can't be bowed anymore.
Certainly not because my old man bent his
too often on any occasion but always to protect us.
Oh well I'm a cripple him they beat down by coincidence.
Mama couldn't endure it didn't want to be with him any more.
Now he stubbornly seeks a moment or a word
on which to hang the next new day
of his life. He's quite an old man now.
On Saturday I think I'll drop in on him
for a moment.

Wounded? (1953-?)

* * *

Słońce jeszcze nie wstało, leży na mokrym piasku.
W porcie skopanej pościeli czuwam i myślę o dziecku.

Jeszcze jest całkiem ciemno między moimi nogami
lecz będę niedługo rodzić. Rodzić do końca dni moich.

Nade mną i pode mną rozrasta się cicha ciemność
jak we mnie korzenie miłości.

Urodzę je, urodzę, przyszyję bluźnierstwem do ciebie
i wtedy pochłonie mnie świt.

Żona? (1950-?)

* * *

The sun's not yet arisen it lies on the wet sand.
In the port of mussed bedsheets I keep watch and think of the child.

It's still completely dark between my legs
but soon I'll give birth. Birthing to the end of my days.

Above me and below me a quiet darkness spreads
like the roots of love inside me.

I'll give birth I'll give birth I'll stitch a blasphemy to you
and then the dawn will swallow me.

Wife? (1950-?)

* * *

Mieszkając w tobie myślę czasem czy rozumiałeś
życia kruchość, tchnienie ucieczki w ruchu planet
i mamy czułość wobec słów
którym wciąż przemywała rany.

To wiem, że jeszcze nie pojąłeś
jak życie się odpycha swoje, jak obco
gaśnie jasny motyw bez słów nucony
by zapomnieć.

Przecież nie mogłeś synu wiedzieć o wojnie czasu
rzeczy śmiechu owianych skrzydłem
błagań lęku dwojga serc skrytych
w twoim śnie.

Wiedzieć musiałeś że świat pęka pod niebosiężnym
zła ramieniem i trzeba skręcić w psalm przepaści
jak serce skręca w uderzeniu
nieobecnego przeznaczenia.

Ojciec? (1927-2003?)

* * *

Living in you I wonder sometimes have you come to understand
the fragility of life the panting of escape into planetary motion
we have a tenderness for words
such as constantly washes clean their wounds.

This I know that you still haven't comprehended
how life repulses its own how strangely
the bright theme is snuffed wordlessly hummed
to forgetfulness.

But you simply couldn't have known my son of the war of time
things laughter shrouded by a wing
pleadings terror of two hearts hidden
in your dreams.

You must have known that the world splits beneath the soaring
arm of evil and that one must swerve quickly into the psalm of the abyss
just as the heart twists in colliding
with an absent destiny.

Father? (1927-2003?)

* * *

Senność, senność, senność, fale kroków gasnące
aniołów idących nago w śnieżnych hełmach ku czołgom.
Cóż, wielu pragnie zobaczyć śmierć i szczęśliwie powrócić.
Żyć i wiedzieć. Zrozumieć co można z umierania.
Wiedzieć, być nieśmiertelnym w ciele wietrznego czasu.

Senność, senność, senność i nuta pustej sieci
bez ryb i obietnic szczęścia.
Z chybocącego pociągu ktoś woła mnie po imieniu.
Chcę wstać, odpowiedzieć. Chcę pobiec
ciepłymi rękami otoczyć
skrzydlaty kształt
boskiej ziemi.

Nie marzę, nie lubię marzyć.
Unosi mnie gorzka senność i przez jej ciężkie bielmo
widzę wyraźnie szczegóły wykute w srebrnym powietrzu:
grzbiety traw poruszone lekkim jak woda ostrzem
kamień w kształcie Afryki z rzekami z białego kwarcu
i żuka jak się gramoli na mariacką wieżę.
Jest już w połowie drogi i powoli brnie wyżej
ku miękkiej łodzi powietrza
w której dzisiaj kończy się zawsze
jutro lub jeszcze dalej.

Zastrzelony? (1950-1970?)

* * *

Sleepiness sleepiness sleepiness the dying waves of steps
of angels walking naked in snowy helmets toward the tanks.
Well, many's the one who wishes to have a glance at death, and then return
alive. To live and know. To understand all that one might of dying.
To know to be immortal in the body of windy time.

Sleepiness sleepiness sleepiness and the note of an empty net
devoid of fish or promises of happiness.
From a bucking train someone calls me by name.
I want to get up and reply. I want to run
to embrace the winged form of the divine earth
with warm arms.

I'm not dreaming I don't like to dream.
I'm in the grip of bitter sleepiness and through its heavy cataract
I see details quite clearly chiselled in the silver air:
the spines of grasses set in motion by a blade as light as water
a rock shaped like Africa with rivers of white quartz
and a beetle crawling up St Mary's steeple.
It's halfway to the top and slowly crawling higher
towards the soft boat of air
in which today is finished forever
tomorrow or later still.

Shot dead? (1950-1970?)

* * *

Czy poezja nie powinna być szczególnie wyczulona na anonimowe niewysłowione przesłanie strawione przez zgiełk śmierci, chaos kłamstwa, wapno niepamięci? Czy ta najbardziej intymna ze sztuk nie powinna użyczać swojego głosu, a umniejszać swoje pragnienia? Zapominać o sobie choćby na mgnienie? Przenikać los ludzi wyblakłych, których żywe pragnienia uwięzły w niejasnej frazie cienia? Czy my, nieustannie zapominani, jesteśmy rozpoznawani przez innych zapomnianych? Co mówią o nas umarli? Czy nas zapamiętali? Czy my wsłuchujemy się w tych, których nie pamiętamy?

Zamordowani na Wybrzeżu w 1970 roku mają swoje imiona, pomniki (choć nie jesteśmy pewni, czy wiemy o wszystkich zamordowanych), istnieją w pamięci przekazywanej w rodzinnym kręgu. Żyją także jako symbol oporu przeciwko nieludzkiej władzy w drugiej połowie XX wieku lub jeden ze śladów jej zbrodniczej działalności. Ostatnio niektórzy ożyli w filmie *Czarny czwartek*. Zastanawiam się, czy nie moglibyśmy podejść bliżej do nich i do tych, których kochali? Wcielić się na wieczny moment w ich trwające i podróżujące, i zmartwychwstałe, i zatarte, i nierozpoznane i wiekuiste, i spopielone, i nienarodzone życie?

* * *

Should poetry not be particularly sensitive to unspoken, anonymous messages digested by the uproar of death, the chaos of lies, the quicklime of oblivion? Should that most intimate of the arts not lend its voice and give solace somewhat to its yearnings? Forget about itself at least for a moment? Penetrate the destinies of persons faded away, whose living desires were snagged on an unclear phrase of shadow? Are we, the constantly forgotten, recognised by other forgotten souls? What do the dead say about us? Do they remember us? Can we listen carefully to those we don't remember?

Those who were murdered on the Baltic coast in 1970 have their names and their monuments (although we can't be sure that we know all of the murdered); they exist in the memories handed down in the family circle. They also live as a symbol of resistance to an inhuman régime in the second half of the twentieth century, or as some of the evidence of its criminal activity. Lately, some of them have been brought to life in the film *Black Thursday*. I wonder if one mightn't approach them any closer, and those whom they loved? To incarnate oneself, for an eternal moment, in their continuing voyage of resurrection, in their effaced and unrecognised and everlasting and unborn life, reduced to ashes?

JAN POLKOWSKI'S *VOICES* — THE ANTIGONES OF THE BALTIC COAST

Jan Polkowski's cycle of poems entitled *Voices* [*Głosy*] has no counterpart in the literature of Poland — or even that of the world. It is not only a volume of poems, but a coherent and thematically homogenous poetic collection, a cycle of eighteen poems dedicated to the victims of the massacre on the Baltic Coast in 1970.

THE ANNIHILATION OF THE POET

The poetic technique employed by Polkowski, which permits him to enter the skin of another person and to speak from within his narrators, is most fully seen in *Voices*, as the volume is constructed of the utterances of the living and deceased victims of December 1970. The poems, composed some forty years after the massacre, transmit this suffering in a poignant fashion, not so much of the murdered, as of their families: the mothers, fathers, siblings or children who remained behind with their loss — the bitter absence of their loved ones. Here, suffering is not merely omnipresent, it is, above all, enduring, stubborn, finding no solace in the passing of daily life. Contrary to the cliché, time heals no wounds.

From a purely technical point of view, the recording of non-existence is the most difficult thing to accomplish, for the suitably chosen poetics must represent nothingness, a concrete vacuum represented by undomesticated feelings, absent gestures, the shades of past love or the experience of unexpressed, yet poignant vacancy, lack — a deficit both physical and psychological. In other words, a convincing form must be found for empathy, so that it should not merely be the private experience of the poet but also become something in which we ourselves participate. Drawing from different Euro-American literary traditions (more of this later), the poet takes advantage of several models of literary expression, like the epigram and the dramatic monologue, in order to create a unique fusion that evokes a moving narrative of suffering.

Above all, Polkowski's *Voices* constitutes a family tragedy so powerful, so moving, that it is only with difficulty that I dare write about these poems. They evoke too great an agitation within me to permit me a facile historical-literary distance from which to analyse the poet's style and his strategy of constructing poetic tension. What is the cornerstone of the greatness of *Voices*? Their theme and their incarnation. The poet draws back into the shadows, surrendering himself to his protagonists as if he were not present at all, so as to disappear within their tortured bodies and maltreated souls. This withdrawal, this shrinking behind his protagonists, is so great that the author's name does not even figure on the cover of the Polish first edition! The graphic suggestion is clear: 'others' are speaking here; I am just a medium. These are 'their' utterances; I only transmit them. This literary modesty, this restraint of the author has been underscored in his public statements. At author's evenings, Polkowski would argue that he 'heard' these poems. This is a very Romantic conception of poetry, and these days, one approaches it with scepticism. Poetry, after all, is a 'working in language' as one says in these latter days. But it must be admitted that it is a conception that is in accord with the general tendency of the poetry of the author of *The Bitter Hour* [Gorzka godzina]. We might also acknowledge that here we are dealing with a poetic manifest of the poetry of human fate, poetry standing to the defence of the individual or — as Wojciech Ligęza somewhat differently puts it — 'lamentational poetry.'[1]

To continue on with ethics and poetics: in *Etyka solidarności*[2] [The Ethics of Solidarity] Fr Józef Tischner explained solidarity by means of images and words taken from the Gospels: 'Bear ye one another's burdens.'[3] In this

---

[1] W. Ligęza, 'Osobny. Spojrzenie na całość' [Personal. A Look at the Whole], in Józef Maria Ruszar, *W mojej epoce już wymieram* [I am Going Extinct in my Own Times]. Kraków: JMR Trans-Atlantyk, 2017, p. 368.

[2] J. Tischner, *Etyka Solidarności* [The Ethics of Solidarity]. Kraków: Znak, 1981.

[3] See Galatians 6:2: Bear ye one another's burdens; and so you shall fulfil the law of Christ.

sense, aiding the victims to express their pain, the poet has incarnated the idea of solidarity: he has taken someone else's burden upon his shoulders. And in the sense of poetic tradition, he has taken on the role of the chorus from *Antigone*. *Voices* constitute an Antigone divided amongst mother, sister, fiancée, wife, brother, father, son — people who love people, who are marked by the memory and pain of loss, of grief directed against the world, and even against the departed, not only against their tormentors and executioners. The fragmentary character of what we know about those who died, and about the living, who are drying up from sorrow, mirrors the imperfect perception of the aching soul, which is too small to contain so much sadness. A social or political tragedy is one thing, and a personal catastrophe is something else: the poignant loss, constantly summoned, and each time from another perspective.

THE ANNIHILATION OF HISTORY

Societal history is rich in events. The name itself indicates their temporality, their ephemerality, their very sliding away into 'historicity.' Meanwhile, personal history rebels against becoming 'history.' It is an endless present. And thus, in human categories — 'eternity.' The impossibility of liberation from pain is one of the basic reasons why the protagonists of the volume express a resentment to the world and to other people. And this resentment is not always directed at the murderers; sometimes, it is addressed to the victims — something that resounds even more tragically, such as in the poem '*** Dearest Daddy how sincerely I hated you [*Son? (1960-?)*]':

> Dearest Daddy how sincerely I hated you
> for you went away and the rest of the world stayed where it was.
> That, and probably too for the pinch of poverty that followed.
> We were helped out by uncle parish neighbours.
> When I was old enough I picked bottles rags and scrap metal.
> We ate stale bread soup hasty pudding potatoes
> potatoes potatoes I hated you
> because you were somewhere else and didn't give a fig for us.
> [1–8]

Here we find the most unexpected tone in the fugue of suffering that is *Voices*. How horrid. In the face of such an experience, we stand helpless. It would seem that the many years of poverty, nagging and humiliating, are crucial here, but actually, the most searing experience is absence: the entire world exists, except the narrator's father! Here we discover the real dimensions of the tragedy. And it is only the final position of the poem that offers hope for an understanding:

> When my hatred cooled I would glance at mama
> who when she wasn't sobbing was sobbing all the more.
> Then the hatred came back making it easier to muddle through.
> I thought you perished because you didn't want
> to drag such heavy loads up against the current
> of grand words and so to be free of them
> you let them shoot you through the heart.
> But maybe you were nothing but a simple coward?
> Poland. I don't know what to say of her.
> I saw her in the closed eyes of my little sister
> and when mama's back suddenly convulsed
> at the sharp turn of the future. In December I threw it all to hell
> mimeographed underground stuff sat in gaol a bit.
> Now I'm a roofer.
> I make roofs for people.
> For a few good years now although not too often
> I visit you in the graveyard.
>
> [9–25]

In any case, the use of the vocative itself leaves us in no doubt that this is a cry of love and despair. Such relations of son to father who, while being non-existent, is still and all ever present, are rich in other paradoxes, such as we find in the poem '*** I don't know what it's like to be an orphan. [*Son? (1957-?)*]:

> I don't know what it's like to be an orphan. Mother, sister
> two brothers — I was fourteen
> when I became my family's father and my own.
>
> [1–3]

What follows is a succinct tale of the necessity of filling the breach in the family constellation, of accelerated maturity, a maturity deprived of a childhood, which results in a flintiness of character, stubbornness in the fight with destiny. And thus the metaphorical conclusion: a vision of an infernal world, in which the narrator determines not to submit to the contrarieties of life and, in a way, vows himself perseverance:

> The sea hammers the poles. The sun grows in the springs.
> People of moist salt run on immovable.
> Fire chases them into alleys closes cold lips.
> I stand over the putrid water at the dirty port's
> shoreline. Never again no one
> will I ever allow to push me over.
>
> [4–9]

What do the victims speak of? What do they complain of? Absence, the impossibility of love's realisation. For there is no experience here of paternal tenderness or filial love, nor will there ever be, for the dream of at least for a while 'sitting down [together] on the sand,'[4] or to experience anything together, even for the most banal moment. The absence of simple, ordinary life, not any extraordinary dream or adventure, it is this that turns out to be the greatest loss. Who can give back a motherhood that never came to be? Who can be rewarded for the lack of a father? The disappearance of a lover? The death of a son?

Paradoxically, as in the poem in which a fourteen-year-old must suddenly become a man, extraordinary reserves of courage appear in the heroes of these poems. Here, the mother of one of the murdered has to go on living, somehow, and cannot allow herself even a moment of weakness, for her husband has died as well. She has remained alone with a gaggle of children, and so, she must be 'tough,' so, she must not 'wallow in the memories' of her son's death, so as not to see her strength flag. From this springs her 'examination of conscience' and her unfounded 'apologies,' the paradoxical needlessness of which so strikes the sensitive reader:

---

[4] Just such a dream is mentioned in the verse '*** The short shift of air following your casual gesture [Father? (1924-2003?)]'.

> I know that you don't blame me. Besides you, I had
> three others. Adaś somewhat stunned at his own existence
> Józio clever as no one yet in all our family
> and Asia who spoke little — proof that goodness exists.
> Father expired quickly and since then I've had trouble
> gathering my thoughts in the darkness. Work queues cooking altering
> clothes. From adults to children from older to younger.
> It seemed that I would never fall asleep just grow cold
> needle in hand thimble on finger macaroni dough
> rolled flat by a shard of my heart. I wanted to die
> from shame that I'm alive. From implacable love from fear
> of your sprawled shadow. Now I'm nearing
> eighty so I guess it's high time for you to forgive me. It was me
> fed with my own body that endless range of helpless
> days. And I know that each one of them killed you over and over again
> my son.[5]

Despite the fact that the last two hundred years of the history of Poland are the history of strong women, raising the children of husbands fallen in battle, the theme of this volume is constituted of individual human tragedies, and not the drama of national denial or the public audacity of murderers, who never answered for the murders they committed on the civilian population (and whom, through the nefariousness of politicians, became 'men of honour'). History, especially that written with a capital letter, has in short been annihilated, and all that remains is the individual human being alone with his individual suffering. This is an unusually rare phenomenon, practically absent from Polish literature on account of its Tyrtaean traditions. After all, individuals do perish in Polish literature, but as individual citizens! They are, therefore, something like the heroes in Homer, members of the *polis*. The Romantic paradigm still resonates in the poetry of the martial law period, to recall just the poem and collection entitled 'Report from the Besieged City'.[6] Meanwhile, as Wojciech Ligęza notes:

---

[5] '*** I know that you don't blame me. [Mother? (1928-2009?)]'

[6] The period in question began on 13 December 1981, with the brutal delegalisation of Solidarity by the government of the Polish People's Republic and lasted until its symbolical lifting on 22 July 1983 —

Polkowski does justice to the individual existence:
Historiography is rather silent concerning the destruction of the cosmos of the family hearth, the ruin of family life, of individual traumas which cannot be removed, and statistics offer only numbers entirely rinsed clean of human existences. It is poetry that allows open access to the dramas undergone by individual persons, although — and this must be emphasised — the revisiting of evil moments in history do not occur all that frequently these days.[7]

These two elements — the incarnation of the author within his narrators, and the negation of history to the benefit of the individual existence — constitute the singularity of this collection in Polkowski's oeuvre, and the unique position of the volume in the history of contemporary Polish literature. This is boldly presented in the poem '*** The Christmas Eve opłatek mama in her ashen dress':

> The Christmas Eve opłatek mama in her ashen dress
> sets down as custom dictates a spare plate
> by the empty chair. Motionless she stares
> right through us and the trembling air the barszcz the fish
> the straw the fir branches right through the frost-covered walls
> to the street of white stone and the bent figure
> falling beneath the weight of unavoidable treachery.
>
> *Brother? (1958-?)*

Let us take note of the word 'treachery' in the concluding line of the poem. This is a subtle allusion to the historical circumstances of an army firing upon its own, unarmed citizens, and the decisions of an anti-Polish government. The setting itself does not exceed the frame of the homey, family, holiday situation. Even the reference to the Polish Christmas Eve tradition

---

the Communist holiday of Poland Reborn (which celebrated the publication, in Moscow, of the manifesto of the Communist controlled Polish Committee of National Liberation). *The Report from the Besieged City* [Raport z oblężonego miasta] was written by Polish poet Zbigniew Herbert, under the impressions of the imposition of martial law. It was published in Paris in 1983.

[7] Ligęza, p. 368.

of setting an extra plate is not, nor must it be, a sub-text dating the massacre at the Baltic Coast, for in reality the people died on 17 December. Furthermore, the scene described in the poem may be taking place many years later. That's even certain, if we take into account the calmness of those present and the emphasis that it is a 'custom' that we are witnessing. Evoking the trivialised ceremony in the context of the absence of the murdered family member, Polkowski subtly raises the temperature of his expression, not by raising, but rather by lowering, his voice. Such a system of 'cooling down' one's language for the description of emotionally strong situations was perfected by Zbigniew Herbert. An additional context, hidden as it were in the background, is the fact that 'as custom dictates,' this additional plate is being set out for a stranger, an unexpected guest, and, actually, God out in search of shelter, in remembrance of the lack of hospitality in Bethlehem. This is neither the first, nor the last example of a transformation of historical categories into ethical and existential ones, in this case — religious ones.

Allusions to political and historical realia are eminently rare and deprived of detail. The last names of those responsible for the massacre are never pronounced. Practically speaking, a person not knowing the history will not know who is being spoken of when one of the mothers says:

My niece says: *I know they killed your son.*
It's over now it only keeps on happening in your poor head.
I know that general gets under your skin in that aureole of glory
he wears but just spit on him.[8]

From the point of view of national history, and the history of Polish literature, these eighteen poems, and so, a modest little volume of poetry, is something of a scandal. Firstly, Polkowski obliterates history, especially that 'grand,' momentous, political history, which likes to be spelt with a capital letter, for we treat the workers' demonstrations as an important stage in the regaining of our social and national liberty. For there can be no doubt about it that the December Events — as incidents of those several days in December 1970 have been termed — belong to the history of Poland and the history of the liberation of those nations enslaved by the Communist empire. For us

---

[8] *** 'I look at my nails — [Mother? (1929-?)].'

Poles, but also for the historical researchers of this part of the world, this is History. Meanwhile, for the protagonists described in these poems, history does not exist. Neither that written with a large, or a small letter. Polkowski's poems obliterate history to the benefit of the individual existence. There is neither the past, nor the past tense, in these poems. There is today, and the present-imperfect tense — or shall we say, a tense endless in its pain. For death has no unitary dimension, and touches also the loved ones of the deceased, those who survived.

As we well know, not once, not twice, but always, from the beginning of history, poetry has celebrated great historical events. A special literary genre — the *epos* — has been developed for the presentation of key episodes in the life of peoples and nations, which memorialises legendary or historical heroes. Furthermore, the memorialisation of history has led to the creation of an individual literary form known as the epic, which constitutes a traditional trinity along with the lyric and the dramatic. The epic, in verse or prose, has won itself the right to concern itself with dramatic events in the life of nations, and the heroes described therein count upon immortality and a name that will be significant for generations. Homer begins his great song with the words:

> Sing, goddess, the anger of Peleus' son Achilleus
> and its devastation, which put pains thousandfold upon the Achaeans,
> hurled in their multitudes to the house of Hades strong souls
> of heroes, but gave their bodies to be the delicate feasting
> of dogs, of all birds, and the will of Zeus was accomplished.[9]

The epic celebrates the victors in the bloody shambles which constitute history. The elevated tone of the narrative is an accepted form of expression, and the immortalisation of the hero's name is the goal. Against such a historical and literary background, *Voices* is a volume of quiet, but firm, resistance. The poet does not celebrate the victors. To speak the truth, nor does he celebrate the heroic vanquished, according to the rule *gloria victis*, which ennobles the fallen, who struggled valiantly against the slings and arrows of fate. This time, poetry shows no concern for the immortality of heroes, but rather, that of the

---

[9] Homer, *Iliad*, I:1-6, translation by Richmond Alexander Lattimore, Chicago: University of Chicago Press, 1961.

most ordinary of people, broken by pain. It does not present the thunderclap of death's blow, but rather tortured individual life. It does not create fierce images of extraordinary acts; rather, it speaks of the arduous struggle with the horrific, never-ending terror of banal everyday life. The heroes are not exceptional; they are rather average, nameless even, so that history would not be able to memorialise them. At any rate, history has no desire to remember them, and anti-heroes assume no place in history, for they have rejected it, enclosing themselves whole in their individual existences, delimited to their closest family members. Their world is the world of their loved ones — the lost. It is the absent ones who rule their everyday life, not the criminal politicians. The poet characterises their drama according to their relation to the deceased; for this reason, each poem is the expression of wife, mother, sister...

THE ANNIHILATION OF THE FUTURE

We note that when the living speak, time disappears. More precisely, essential time disappears, for that marked by the calendar, of course, never stops, and is merely transformed into an unimportant eternity. In such a petrified time (somewhat similar to the eternal return of the same known from anthropology, or St Augustine's 'eddies in time'), the repetition of gestures is both necessary (in the sense of: forced, imposed, perhaps maniacal) and unimportant, for they are deprived of any essential sense:

> I look at my nails —
> painted unevenly.
> I paint them every day wipe the polish off paint them again.
> Paint wipe paint.
> Morning Mass and my fingernails alone keep me in one
> piece.[10]

Everything important that was to have happened, has already occurred. The rest is meaningless, and the 'working-class Lady Macbeth' behaves as if her obsessive behaviour was symptomatic of an obsessive-compulsive disorder, to use medical terminology. It's a different matter with the murdered, whose lives

---

[10] '*** *I look at my nails* — [Mother? (1929-?)],' 1-6.

have reached their accomplishment, if too prematurely. When it is those who were shot that are under consideration, the accent falls on lives unfulfilled, and not on the dramatic death itself. For here we are speaking of consequences, not any single fact. Now, the murdered person will not achieve anything, and certainly will not experience anything anymore. As Wojciech Ligęza writes, 'we associate interrupted life with a breach in existence as a whole; the death of an individual, on the other hand, is a private end of the world.'[11] For the evil of the killing is always found in the fact that it deprives a person of the future. 'It's hard to sum up all the magical incarnations,' says one of the murdered[12] upon counting up all of his boyhood dreams and games, brought to an end by a rifle round shot off in the direction of a Tri-Cities[13] queue. We know that there will be no further incarnations, and that the number has become finite. The definitiveness of killing is one of the themes expressed by those shot, although posthumous reflections on the theme of their lives up to that point are not lacking (and here we find an affinity with the genre of the epitaph, to which theme we will shortly return), as well as a brooding on happiness experienced up to the fatal moment ('*** With transparent hands [*Shot dead? (1948-1970)*]'):

> With transparent hands you made me sandwiches.
> Blindly, you plunged your knife into the quiet sea.
> You made me sandwiches you sliced the earthly globe
> into neat even pieces. You stuffed my canvas
> knapsack with hours of separation.
> You wrapped the children's faces in grey paper.
> You stroked my cheek as if I were going off to war
> as if the door was made of fire and not of fibreboard.
> Later, I made my careful way into the electricians' lockers
> and unfolded the paper to watch you slowly disappearing.

Ordinary, wordless gestures, constituting the comfort of hours of absence — here we have a description of married tenderness that evades emotional em-

---

[11] Ligęza, p. 370.
[12] '*** Squall. In a cold shirt I walk along the bay. [*Shot Dead? (1954-1970?)*].'
[13] In Polish, the metropolitan area Gdańsk-Gdynia-Sopot is referred to as the *Trójmiasto*.

phasis. The whole volume, after all, is composed of quite words, ordinary, calm, grey and transparent, as it were, deprived of the bizarre. The murdered themselves do not complain; they merely present facts. One poem — also a soliloquy — forms a category of its own. It is expressed by a wounded man who, himself physically paralysed, reveals his intention of visiting his aged father — who has been mentally paralysed, a person who submitted to the government (for the benefit of his children) now mentally broken by the tragedy of the wounding of his son. In a certain sense, here it is the father who is dead, or perhaps only more of a cripple than his invalid son. As Przemysław Dakowicz incisively notes: 'The living resemble the dead even more than those who perished. These are people who have been hollowed out, always looking behind them, even if they stubbornly insist the opposite, like the eighty-year-old mother of one of the killed.[14]

VOICES AND THE LITERARY TRADITION

Polkowski's *Voices* are an exceptional phenomenon, not only in Polish literature, but also that of the world. We have here a distinct, persona poetic voice, which has no literary counterpart and yet — like every other literary text — it did not arise in a vacuum. We can find some similarities to other literary genres, but at the same time, these but further underscore the essential differences wherewith *Voices* breaks through the conventions of existing tradition.

THE EPIGRAM TRADITION

Polkowski's verse might be read in the context of the *Palatine Anthology*[15] in the Polish versions of Zygmunt Kubiak, the prominent translator and human-

---

[14] P. Dakowicz, 'Na marginesie *Głosów* Jana Polkowskiego (kartki wydarte z notatnika)' [In the Margins of Jan Polkowski's *Voices* (Pages Torn from a Notebook)], in Józef Maria Ruszar, *W mojej epoce już wymieram* [I am Going Extinct in my Own Times]. Kraków: JMR Trans-Atlantyk, 2017, p. 221.

[15] A collection of Greek epigrams spread across many centuries. It was discovered in 1606 in the Palatine Library in Heidelberg, after which it is named. The Polish classicist Zygmunt Kubiak published a selection in his own translation in 1978 (most recently in 2002); in English, a short selection of one hundred poems was published by Dudley Fitts in 1935.

ist, for whom Polkowski has great respect, as his many references to him in prose[16] and poetry as well testify.[17]

Ancient Greek epigrams, carved into funereal steles, were composed by such remarkable authors as Archilochus, Sappho, Simonides and Anacreon, and, as Kubiak writes, constitute 'a peculiar type of poetry — extremely fastidious and concise [...] eloquent with silence as well as words.'[18] Funereal inscriptions beg the passer-by of a prayer or a moment of reflection. In the Hellenistic world they became an important literary genre, which — in contrast to the epic — concerned itself more with the unique, personal, and often lonely fate of the individual, and not the history of a citizen of the *polis*, as takes place in the epics of Homer.

These two collections are linked by a strange kinship. The terseness of the epigram, and its concern with everyday life, is where we find this similarity. The funereal nature of the work, in which, generally speaking, the dead address the living, constitutes the difference between them, since, in general, the narrators of the poems in *Voices* are generally living persons (12) remembering the dead (5). It is people speaking here, not steles. They are something on the order of living gravestones, recalling the death of their loved ones. Human 'voices' are important here, not 'inscriptions' ('inscription — *epigram* in ancient Greek'). Among the ancient epigrams (funereal 'inscriptions') as Zygmunt Kubiak emphasises, we find, of course, collective and heroic inscriptions, sometimes dedicated to important persons, although private pain also takes voice, such as Andronicus' 'Mother's Lament:' 'Bid farewell amidst tears, you departed for the gloomy fields beyond the Acheron, my sweet Democratea, leaving your mother nothing but lament. And she — when you died, my daughter — took in hand the freshly-sharpened iron, and shaved her head of her grey hair.'[19] In another place, the departed himself takes voice — namelessly: 'Here I

---

[16] See: J. Polkowski, 'Europa to bezdomność' [Europe is Homelessness], in *Polska moja miłość* [Poland my Love]. Warsaw: Pro-Patria, 2014, pp. 233-240.

[17] See the poem 'Hymn' (from the volume *Cień* [Shadow]), 'Pamięci Zygmunta Kubiaka' [In Memoriam Zygmunt Kubiak], J. Polkowski, *Gdy Bóg się waha. Poezje 1977-2017* [When the Lord Hesitates. Poems 1977-2017]. Kraków: Instytut Myśli Józefa Tischnera JMR Trans-Atlantyk, 2017, p. 265.

[18] *Palatine Anthology*, p. 10.

[19] *Palatine Anthology*, p. 112.

lie, unfortunate one, slain by an armed bandit. I lie here, lamented by no one.'[20]

And so: similarities and differences. The anonymity of the victims and the mourners is a characteristic trait of Polkowski's poems, whereas in the *Palatine Anthology* — it is merely coincidental. Among the eighteen poems of *Voices* only five are the expressions of the departed, and only four are epigrams. The remainder are rather long considering the general tendency of the genre.[21]

THE DRAMATIC MONOLOGUE TRADITION

The inscriptions found on headstones developed into a model of poetic expression, which some dozens of centuries later would be called the 'dramatic monologue.'[22] This genre is a sort of lyrical expression in which the poet speaks, not own his own voice, but with that of a persona he creates and entrusts with the role of narrator. The greatest master of the contemporary dramatic monologue is the British poet Robert Browning (1812-1889).[23] His imitators in the twentieth century are, among others, Ezra Pound and T. S. Eliot in English, Constantine Cavafy in Greek, and Czesław Miłosz and Zbigniew Herbert in Poland. The narrative persona among the Polish poets does not derive in a straight line from Browning,[24] as from his twentieth century

---

[20] *Palatine Anthology*, p. 319.

[21] The first expression of a deceased person, '*** Squall. In a cold shirt I walk along the bay. [*Shot Dead? (1954-1970?)*]' exceeds by its length the generic frame which is terse by definition.

[22] The name is associated with the style of Robert Browning and finds its best expression in the volumes *Men and Women* (1855) and *Dramatis personae* (1864), the title of which refers to the custom of listing the characters of a play at the head of the published dramatic work. All of the poems found in this volume are monologues expressed by narrators taking a lyrical role. The monologues of Browning, among the narrators of which we find historical personages and fictional artists, basically constitute a fundamental question of the role played by the personal experiences of witnesses to historical events in the past, and the place thereof in the understanding of history and the conception of the mission of art. This latter especially touches upon the 'expressions' of Renaissance artists — 'Andrea del Sarto,' for example.

[23] The tradition of the dramatic monologue is, of course, much older. It can be found among the Baroque poets such as the great metaphysical poet John Donne. Cf his 'To his Mistress, Going to Bed.'

[24] See E. A. Howe, *The Dramatic Monologue*. New York: Twayne, 1996; A. Sinfield, *Dramatic Monologue*. London: Methuen, 1977; R. Langbaum, *The Poetry of Experience: The Dramatic Monologue in Literary* Tradition. London: Chatto & Windus, 1957. Writing of the narrative persona in the early verse of Zbigniew Herbert, with reference to Longbaum, Stanisław Barańczak turns our attention to the use of the term 'monolog dramatyczny' by Adam Czerniawski, an émigré Polish poet and translator of Herberta. See Barańczak's *Uciekinier z Utopii. O poezji Zbigniewa Herberta* [Refugee from Utopia. On the Poetry of Zbigniew Herbert]. Wrocław, PWN, 2001, p. 169.

poetic descendants.[25] In Polish, it was Herbert who perfected the genre, beginning with his early lyrics such as 'Tren Fortynbrasa' [Fortinbras' Lament] and 'Powrót prokonsula' [The Return of the Proconsul] (*Studium przedmiotu* [Object Study], 1961), up to and including his *Pan Cogito* cycle, as well as later verses, such as 'Damastes z przydomkiem Prokrustes mówi' [Damastes alias Procrustes Speaks'] (*Report from the Besieged City*, 1983).

However much we have to do with literary, mythological or historical personages in the poetry of Herbert, sometimes of ancient provenance (for example, the Roman emperors 'Caligula' or the 'Divine Claudius,' the narrators in *Voices* are homogeneous and anonymous, whose identities are only assumed to be who they are. The individual poems are untitled — which might otherwise have enabled us to suspect who it is that is speaking. They are outfitted only in a sort of 'caption' or 'note' following the monologues, ending in question marks, which suggest that the author merely 'suspects' who it is that is speaking, such as a mother, a fiancée, a son, or someone else related to the given victim. In five of these poems, it is suggested that it is the murdered person speaking. This anonymity, or if you will, scant signification of the characters, is the most important trait of these monologues. We know nothing about them beyond the supposed year of their birth (and, eventually, their death) as well as their purported relationship with the victims. Such 'biographical data' only deepen their alienation with History written with a capital 'H.' Their tragedy, pain and loss do not belong to history at all, but rather to strictly private life, to personal experience. It is true that we are dealing with a certain generation, but there is a lack of social or national background. Indeed, if not or our familiarity of contemporary history and the (unsigned) author's 'Afterword,' the reader might have no clue that the cycle revolves around the December 1970 massacre. Przemysław Dakowicz turns our attention to one more significance of this approach:

> The characters who speak in the works of Polkowski have not been outfitted in concrete names, such as we find in Edgar Lee Masters' works. Everything we know about them is contained in the brief notes that follow each poem. This is a fragmentary knowledge, a suggestion touching upon,

---

[25] Chiefly Eliot, it would seem. During the Occupation, Miłosz translated his *Waste Land* and 'Journey of the Magi,' as well as some poems by Cavafy.

firstly, direct or indirect participation in the tragedy, which the Communist régime euphemistically referred to under the name 'The December Events.' And so we read: 'shot dead,' 'wounded,' 'mother,' 'father,' 'fiancée,' 'wife,' 'son,' 'brother.' Secondly, we have the assumed dates of their birth and (eventually) death. I write 'suggestion' and 'assumed' since each of these bits of information has been outfitted in a question mark, as if the poet wished to make us conscious of the fact that even the most attentive 'listening' to the voices of the past guarantee us no certainty of their proper interpretation. Polkowski seems to argue that we are merely participating in an attempt to penetrate and understand the 'destinies of persons faded away, whose living desires were snagged on the unclear phrases of shadows.'[26]

As a literary ploy, the dramatic monologue has served various ends. Browning used it for the creation of an unbiassed observer, liberated from the snares of Romantic subjectivism. His goal was to provide a voice to a protagonist (especially a historical one) and arousing the reader's sympathy for him, his empathy, and even leading him to a suspension of his moral judgement or — to speak frankly — his condemnation, in the case of protagonists stained with murder (see, for example, *The Ring and the Book*) or that of a lascivious monk.[27] To the extent to which Browning employed the dramatic monologue for the presentation of the subjective opinions of his characters (and in a manner of speaking, for the defence of such reasons) Herbert, on his part, masterfully imported the model in order to discredit his protagonist, who commits the 'irony of self-betrayal.'[28]

In such a context, again we see similarities and differences. The similarities hang on the arousal of sympathy and the employment of the model to present the protagonists' opinions. The differences are based on their historical insignificance, their anonymity. All of the verses in *Voices* are dramatic monologues, which means that *de facto* they function as camouflaged dialogues that

....

[26] Dakowicz, p. 218.
[27] Especially in the case of Renaissance artists. See 'Fra Lippo Lippi.'
[28] This term of D.C. Muecke's (see *The Compass of Irony*. London, 1969, p. 92) was popularised in Herbert studies by Stanisław Barańczak (see *Uciekinier z Utopii*, p. 159). Jan Błoński was first to point out Herbert's varied deployment of irony ('Tradycja, ironia i głębsze znaczenie' [Tradition, Irony, and Deeper Meaning], *Poezja*, 1970, No. 3), after which many other authors followed in his footsteps.

do not take into account the expression of the second person.²⁹ In principle, the living converse with the dead, addressing him directly, and the reader is indirectly informed of this conversation, as if 'he were eavesdropping on a family discussion.' As Wojciech Ligęza puts it:

> Between the worlds an exchange of words and memories is occurring. The murdered seem to bear the living, and the dead are dying countless times in the bodies of the living. That 'Black Thursday' of 17 December 1970 repeats throughout the years — on ordinary Thursdays, and the bloody episode, transferred into the human interior, is transformed into a long process of remembering and brooding on loss.³⁰

THE *SPOON RIVER* TRADITION

Przemysław Dakowicz was the first to draw our attention to the similarities of *Voices* to *The Spoon River Anthology*,³¹ simultaneously stressing the fundamental differences between the two works.³²

The first differentiation concerns the narrative personae. To the extent that the dead in Masters' work basically speak from the perspective of their lives (here we have the epigram tradition, and a resemblance to the *Palatine Anthology*), in Polkowski's volume the voice is given primarily to the living. Even the dead don't so much attempt a summation of their lives (as one finds in epigrams) as much as they concern themselves with the life unlived, the biography unfulfilled — something that partially arises from the fact that we are dealing with people who were murdered young. We have already spoken of the anonymity of the victims (the living as well as the dead, for the former are doubtlessly victims as well).

The protagonists of Masters' anthology are quite concrete. Not only do they possess names (fictional, but that's beside the point), but they are often

---

[29] This procedure is noted in encyclopaedic entries. See Michał Głowiński, 'Monolog dramatyczny' [Dramatic Monologue], Michał Głowiński, Teresa Kostkiewiczowa, Aleksandra Okopień-Sławińska, Janusz Sławiński, eds. *Słownik terminów literackich* [Dictionary of Literary Terminology]. Wrocław: Ossolineum, 2002.

[30] Ligęza, p. 369.

[31] The Polish version of Edgar Lee Masters' most famous work was translated by Michał Sprusiński: *Antologia Spoon River*. Warsaw, 1981.

[32] Dakowicz, pp. 207-232.

related to one another, or their fates are joined like cogs in the wheel of their small-town community, in which everyone knows everybody. They represent the richness of interaction in a small community and narrate its complicated history over the space of a few dozen years. What is lacking here? Thanks to the garrulity of the dead, we come to know an entire provincial universe: a factory of tinned food, the bankruptcy of the local bank, the Civil War and Prohibition, marital infidelity (both open and hidden), divorces, family happiness and romances nipped in the bud, petty deceptions and the large frauds of the powerful, activities in the wings and barefaced lying. Judges and criminals speak here, murderers and the murdered, the wronged and those who wronged them, blasphemers and pastors. Somewhat like we find in the *Palatine Anthology*, which was a pattern for the *Spoon River Anthology*,[33] we come to know human greed, envy, resentment, cruelty, stupidity, and — more rarely — nobility, wisdom, and love, both fulfilled and unfulfilled. In reality, only one trait is common to all the protagonists: an unfulfilled life, a life lost, even if one speaks here and there of 'success' in life.

From this perspective, the protagonists of *Voices* are more homogenous, although 'representative' also, in some way, of their community. And yet the difference is a clear one. First of all, their troubles are not of the banal, bourgeois sort but immense family tragedies; unmerited catastrophes that unexpectedly fell upon the protagonists independent of their good or ill will or their noble or villainous acts. Second, the differentiation exclusively touches upon familial relations, and the range of experiences here is basically confined within familial bounds.

Wojciech Ligęza turns our attention to one more difference:

> *Voices* is, to a certain degree, a Baltic Coast equivalent of the *Spoon River Anthology*, in the sense that the dead are self-representative; they speak of trivial, everyday matters, sketching fragments of a biography, evaluating their hopes and dreams from beyond the grave. But the polyphony created by Masters refers to ordinary lives, untouched by the paroxysms of history. Sudden death from the bullets of the People's Army, on the other

---

[33] References in the *Spoon River Anthology* to antiquity are not lacking and are often direct.

hand, is something quite different — an interruption, a sudden deception, a treacherous blow[34].

In a certain sense, the persons of this drama are also more one-dimensional, which is to say that they are all untied by the same sort of misfortune, although they experience it each in their own way, dependent on their age, gender, as well as relation to the murdered person. Finally, a difference is found in their relation to death. Wojciech Kudyba speaks of this in the following manner:

> To the fundamental differences pointed out by critics, I would add another fact, that the image of death in the volume *Spoon River* is one-dimensional. Masters' protagonists look upon death from the perspective of a dead person, whereas with Polkowski we are dealing with a much broader comprehension, the bold appearance of many perspectives on how death can be viewed, and thus, with a significant broadening of cognitive horizons.[35]

And further:

> Thus, each of the protagonists in *Voices* speaks to us about his own pain. And each one expresses himself a little differently — in accord with his life experiences, mentality, temperament, sex and character. In this way we come to recognise various ways of living through traumas. Polkowski's volume is its own sort of poetic study of the experience of suffering.[36]

The analogies to Masters' work give rise to another question, of the ontological status of the protagonists of the volumes under comparison. This has nothing to do with the fact that these characters are fictional — there can be no question of that. The matter touches upon, rather, the delicate problem of the creation of the literary illusion and so-called 'realism.' In *Spoon River*, the 'realistically' created character are to create the illusion of the sociological

---

[34] Ligęza, p. 369.
[35] W. Kudyba, 'O "Głosach" Jana Polkowskiego' [On Jan Polkowski's *Voices*], in Józef Maria Ruszar, *W mojej epoce już wymieram* [I am Going Extinct in my Own Times]. Kraków: JMR Trans-Atlantyk, 2017, p. 205.
[36] Kudyba, p. 206.

reality of the represented world. They have been imagined in such a way to fit in with the reader's concepts of the province and its bourgeois problems. In this sense, the persons are 'characteristic' and 'authentic,' because they dovetail with the reader's opinions, habits and experiences (at bottom, we are speaking here of the naive, general understanding of 'realism'). The realism of Polkowski's poetry has another character: above all, a psychological one, and the ontological status of the characters is described in another way. Wojciech Kudyba has written insightfully of this:

> The general character of our information concerning the protagonists of the particular works, as well as the question marks that accompany this information is interpreted by the critic on an epistemological level — as symptoms of the difficulties in arriving at the truth, signs of the impossibility of grasping it in its entirety, and uncertainty of a proper interpretation of the facts. It's hard not to agree with this. The author of the volume has taken great pains to deprive his characters of schematisation; an aura of mystery washes over them. He does not allow us to forget that we know only so much of them as they have revealed to us, and we cannot be sure that we've understood them correctly. He is constantly implying to us that we come to know others only to a certain degree and through a coming close to them, and therefore, we can draw near them, sure, but we'll never be capable of fully coming to know them.
>
> Despite this, it seems that the schematisation of the above-mentioned data might possess one more function. The cognitive area is not the only one in this volume that places the reader before problems difficult to solve. [...]
>
> For no less difficult seems to be the ontological status of the characters presented in the book, in other words, their relation to the actually living (or equally, actually dead) participants in the events of the past. It is obvious that *Voices* are peopled by fictional characters, created by the writer. For those who remember the tragedy in Gdańsk, for those, who knew the killed or are in contact with their families, it is equally obvious that the verses created by the poet strive to grasp the experiences of people actually existing, non-fictional persons. And so the lack of personal details of the protagonists might, as I see it, also, and even above all, serve to underscore

this peculiar ambiguity. The poet seems to be saying, 'I'm not a reporter, my poems are not fragments of any interview. But this does not mean that the fictional reality I have created has no connection to the real world.' We can put it another way, too: although the volume is peopled by fictional characters, each of them expresses a certain fragment of the truth about actual reality. In this book, the literary fiction becomes a sort of allusion to the real world.

In our attempt at an even more detailed description of the ontological status of the protagonists of the book, we might therefore say that they are representatives of actually existing people. The idea of representation would mean in that case not only a connection between the literary fiction and historical truth, but also the process of literary generalisation. The poet strives to create a figure that would constitute a certain sociological type and refer to many real persons. For this very reason in presenting said figure, he speaks exclusively of his or her societal role — mother, father, or brother — as well as of a sense of his or her belonging to a certain generation described by the year of birth and, eventually, death. It is characteristic that all of these captions are outfitted in question marks, which sort of additionally reminds us of the fact that the process of evoking that, which we recognise as representative, is a process to a certain degree subjective, in connection with the case of the writer striving to make of fiction an instrument for the proclamation of truth.[37]

Masters does not conceal the fact that all of the characters in his book are entirely fictional, that is, imagined and conventional. Polkowski attempts to suggest, delicately, that although his protagonists belong to a literary fiction, they still represent a historical, sociological and psychological truth, and that lending a voice to characters so constructed is a question of doing justice to real people afflicted with real suffering. The poetic volume is, therefore, no mere literary game or literary concept. At the conclusion of the volume, the poet introduces a short explanation of his intentions:

Those who were murdered on the Baltic coast in 1970 have their names and their monuments (although we can't be sure that we know of all the

---

[37] Kudyba, pp. 203-204.

murdered); they exist in the memories handed down in the family circle. They also live as a symbol of resistance to the inhuman government of the second half of the twentieth century, or as one of the traces of its criminal activity. Lately, some of them have been brought to life in the film *Black Thursday*. I wonder if one mightn't approach them any closer, and those whom they loved? To incarnate oneself, for an eternal moment, in their continuing voyage of resurrecting, in their effaced and unrecognised and everlasting unborn life, reduced to ashes?

The historical context of the volume is constituted by a concrete historical event: the brutal intervention of the Communist army and militia during the workers' protests on the Baltic Coast. A few hundred people[38] were murdered in cold blood; those killed were buried in secret, often under the cover of night and in unmarked graves, and all memory of the crime was expunged.

* * *

They took me to the graveyard they wanted to bury the body.
And from that time on each night the same ritual. He looked
as if they'd sewn him together from unmatching parts. Quick
quick they closed the lid. The wind dragged in rain
from the sea and got tangled in the net of darkened ashes.
You could hear the drops battering the spades
the spades battering the ground screeching against the rocks.
Someone else walked away from the well in the Samaritan woman's flesh.
I remained. Like water. Dumb as an empty
jug.

('*** They took me to the graveyard [*Wife? (1950-?)*]')

Ten years later, the next workers' uprising in the series, this time a victorious one, led to the erection of monuments in several coastal towns in Poland. The most well-known of these was raised on Solidarity Square in Gdańsk, near Gate 2 of the Gdańsk Shipyards (once named for Lenin). Forty years after

---

[38] The régime confirmed the death of only forty-one people.

the massacre, the poet raised his own monument in honour of the shipyard workers and their families, one, as the literary tradition suggests, 'more durable than brass.'[39]

*

Jan Polkowski's *Voices* is an achievement that belong amongst the greatest poetic works written in Polish. Its literary power derives not so much from a deeply felt experience of national history, as much as a strong solidarity with the families of the murdered. This last fact is unusually important, because it stretches past the borders of Poland and beyond the year 1970, which for billions of the inhabitants of our globe is an insignificant date. There is no reason why anyone from Asia, South America or even in Europe knew or experienced a massacre in some unknown city on the shores of a cold sea. But criminal régimes can be found everywhere, and the experience of evil is common to all, just as is the mourning of the slain. The pain of loss is our common heritage no matter where we live. Bare suffering, stripped of historical and local details, is understandable to all. May this experience of the lack of one's loved ones, resurrected by the power of Polkowski's expressive talent, bring catharsis and the aesthetic comfort of all great poetry. Such, after all, was the author's intent.

Józef Maria Ruszar

---

[39] Jan Polkowski, *Głosy* [Voices]. Sopot: Biblioteka TOPOSu, 2012.

BIBLIOGRAPHY

PRIMARY SOURCES

POLKOWSKI, Jan. *Gdy Bóg się waha. Poezje 1977-2017* [When the Lord Hesitates. Poems 1977-2017]. Kraków: Instytut Myśli Józefa Tischnera JMR Trans-Atlantyk, 2017.

POLKOWSKI, Jan. *Głosy* [Voices]. Sopot: Biblioteka TOPOSu, 2012.

SECONDARY SOURCES

BARAŃCZAK, Stanisław. *Uciekinier z Utopii. O poezji Zbigniewa Herberta* [Refugee from Utopia. On the Poetry of Zbigniew Herbert]. Wrocław: PWN, 2001.

DAKOWICZ, Przemysław. 'Na marginesie *Głosów* Jana Polkowskiego (kartki wydarte z notatnika)' [In the Margins of Jan Polkowski's *Voices* (Pages Torn from a Notebook)], in RUSZAR.

GŁOWIŃSKI, Michał. ed., et al. *Słownik terminów literackich* [Dictionary of Literary Terminology]. Wrocław: Ossolineum, 2002.

HERBERT, Zbigniew. *Raport z oblężonego miasta* [Report from the Besieged City]. Paris: Instytut Literacki, 1983.

HOWE, Elizabeth A. *The Dramatic Monologue*. New York: Twayne, 1996.

KUDYBA, Wojciech. 'O "Głosach" Jana Polkowskiego' [On Jan Polkowski's *Voices*], in RUSZAR.

LANGBAUM, Robert. *The Poetry of Experience: The Dramatic Monologue in Literary Tradition*. London: Chatto & Windus, 1957.

LIGĘZA, Wojciech. 'Osobny. Spojrzenie na całość' [Personal. A Look at the Whole], in RUSZAR.

MUECKE, Douglas C. *The Compass of Irony*. London: Methuen, 1969.

POLKOWSKI, Jan. 'Europa to bezdomność' [Europe is Homelessness], in *Polska moja miłość* [Poland my Love]. Warsaw: Pro-Patria, 2014.

RUSZAR, Józef Maria. *W mojej epoce już wymieram* [I am Going Extinct in my Own Times]. Kraków: JMR Trans-Atlantyk, 2017.

SINFIELD, Alan. *Dramatic Monologue*. London: Methuen, 1977.

TISCHNER, Józef. *Etyka Solidarności* [The Ethics of Solidarity]. Kraków: Znak, 1981.

ABOUT THE AUTHOR

Jan Polkowski (born 1953) is a poet and a prose writer. During the Communist years, he worked as a publisher and editor in the Polish underground press system. After Poland's regaining of independence in 1989, he was publisher and editor of the newspaper *Czas Krakowski* [The Kraków Times].

As a poet, Polkowski debuted in 1978 with several poems in the uncensored literary quarterly, *Zapis* [The Record]. His first volume, *To nie jest poezja* [This is not Poetry], was printed two years later, in 1980, by the Niezależna Oficyna Wydawnicza NOWA [NOWA Independent Publishers], which makes him the only Polish poet to have debuted in the underground press system. His subsequent volumes were also printed by independent publishers: *Oddychaj głęboko* [Breathe Deeply (1981)], *Ogień. Z notatek 1982-1983* [Fire. Personal Writings 1982-1983 (1983)], *Drzewa* [Trees (1986)].

Polkowski was interned at the imposition of martial law on 13 December 1981. Upon his release from prison in 1983, he went on to serve as editor of the underground social and literary magazine, *Arka* [The Ark]. In the same year, he won one of the most prestigious Polish literary prizes — the Geneva-based Kościelski Foundation Award. His first legally published volume, *Elegie z Tymowskich Gór* [Elegies from the Tymowskie Mountains (Znak)], came out in 1990 and contained a selection of pieces that had already appeared in print, as well as previously unpublished poems from the early period of his career.

Several years of publishing silence ensued, after which Polkowski finally made his literary comeback in 2009 with *Cantus*, which volume won the Andrzej Kijowski Prize in 2010. He followed this up with two more collections: *Cień* [Shadow (2010)] and *Głosy* [Voices (2012)]. This latter publication won him the 'Orpheus' Konstanty Ildefons Gałczyński Award for Poetry. In 2015, Polkowski published *Gorzka godzina* [The Bitter Hour], consisting of poems written in the village of Tymowa, where he had settled not long before. Another collection, *Gdy Bóg się waha. Poezje 1977-2017*

[When God Wavers. Poems 1977-2017], came out in 2017, after which several more books followed in quick succession: *Pochód duchów* [A Procession of Ghosts (1918)], *Rozmowy z Różewiczem* [Conversations with Różewicz (2018)], *Łyżka ojca* [My Father's Spoon (2021)], and *Pomieszane języki* [A Confusion of Tongues (2021)].

In 2013, Polkowski debuted as a novelist with *Ślady krwi. Przypadki Henryka Harsynowicza* [Bloodstains. The Trials of Henryk Harsynowicz], which won the Identitas Award in 2014. A collection of his short prose pieces, *Portier i inne opowiadania* [The Janitor and Other Stories], was published in 2019, followed, a year later, by a volume of daily reflections, entitled *Pandemia i inne plagi* [The Pandemic and Other Plagues].

In 2014, Polkowski also published a collection of journalistic pieces, *Polska, moja miłość* [Poland, My Love], and in 2019, an autobiography in the form of a book-length interview conducted by Piotr Legutko, entitled *Ryzyko bycia Polakiem* [The Risk of Being Polish].

The present volume, *Voices,* has also been translated into German, Romanian, Ukrainian and Russian.

LIST OF WORKS BY JAN POLKOWSKI

To nie jest poezja [This is not Poetry]. Warsaw: Niezależna Oficyna Wydawnicza NOWA, 1980.

Oddychaj głęboko [Breathe Deeply]. Kraków: ABC, 1981.

Ogień. Z notatek 1982-1983 [Fire. From my Notebooks: 1982-1983]. Kraków: Półka Poetów, 1983.

Drzewa. Wiersze 1983-1987 [Trees. Poems 1983-1987]. Kraków: Oficyna Literacka, 1987.

Elegie z Tymowskich Gór, 1988-1989 [Elegies from the Tarnów Hills, 1988-1989]. Kraków: Wydawnictwo Literackie, 2008.

Cantus. Kraków: Wydawnictwo a5, 2009.

Cień [Shadow]. Kraków: Znak, 2010.

Głosy [Voices]. Sopot: Biblioteka Toposu, 2012.

Ślady krwi. Przypadki Henryka Harsynowicza [Traces of Blood. The Cases of Henryk Harsynowicz]. Kraków: Wydawnictwo M, 2013.

Polska moja miłość [Poland, my Love]. Warsaw: Wydawnictwo Pro Patria, 2014.

Gorzka godzina [The Bitter Hour]. Warsaw: Wydawnictwo Sic!, 2015.

Pochód duchów [A Parade of Spirits]. Sopot: Biblioteka Toposu, 2018.

Rozmowy z Różewiczem [Conversations with Różewicz]. Kraków: PWM, 2018.

Portier i inne opowiadania [The Porter and Other Stories]. Sopot-Kraków: TOPOS and Instytut Literatury, 2019.

Ryzyko bycia Polakiem, z Janem Polkowskim rozmawia Piotr Legutko [The Risk of Being Polish. Piotr Legutko in Conversation with Jan Polkowski]. Kraków: Instytut Literatury, 2019.

Pandemia i inne plagi [Pandemia and Other Plagues]. Warsaw-Kraków: Volumen and Instytut Literatury, 2020.

Łyżka ojca [My Father's Spoon]. Warsaw: Wydawnictwo Sic!, 2021.

ABOUT THE TRANSLATOR

Charles S. Kraszewski (born 1962) is a literary translator from Polish, Czech, and Slovak. He is the author of four volumes of original poetry; three in English (*Beast, Diet of Nails*, and *Chanameed*) and one in Polish (*Hallo, Sztokholm*). He has also published a satirical novel (*Accomplices, You Ask?*).

LIST OF PHOTOGRAPHS BY MARIA GĄSECKA

'Stocznia Gdańska. Zamknięte' . . . . cover
'Kuźnia Gdańska' 6
'Opuszczona Stocznia Gdańska (1)'' 12-13
'Opuszczona Stocznia Gdańska (2)' 16-17
'Opuszczona Stocznia Gdańska (3)' 24-25
'Głosy (1)' 32-33
'Nabrzeże Stoczni Gdańskiej' 44-45
'Głosy (3)' 56-57
'Głosy (2)' 60
'Nabrzeże Stoczni Gdańskiej (2)' 84

ABOUT THE PHOTOGRAPHER

Maria Gąsecka was born in 1982. She is a graduate of the Polish Higher School of Film, Theatre and Television in Łódź and Norwich University of the Arts. She collaborated in such documentary films as *Herman Goering Karierre, Ku chwale ojczyzny* [In Praise of the Fatherland], *Czarny czwartek, dlaczego?* [Black Thursday, why?]. She has worked as a cinematic still photographer; she is the author of a series of photographs and exhibits: Sport Photography (2006, 2007), Closer (2011), Mute (2011, 2013), Gates and Doors — Gdańsk (2013), Magic Doors (2013), Cool Days on the Baltic Sea (2014). She curated the one-day no-gallery exhibition Two Coasts (2019). She is curator and author of the exhibition, as well as author of the collage What Created Me (2021).

Olanda
by Rafał Wojasiński

I've been happy since the morning. Delighted, even. Everything seems so splendidly transient to me. That dust, from which thou art and unto which thou shalt return — it tempts me. And that's why I wander about these roads, these woods, among the nearby houses, from which waft the aromas of fried pork chops, chicken soup, fish, diapers, steamed potatoes for the pigs; I lose my eye-sight, and regain it again. I don't know what life is, Ola, but I'm holding on to it. Thus speaks the narrator of Rafał Wojasiński's novel *Olanda*. Awarded the prestigious Marek Nowakowski Prize for 2019, *Olanda* introduces us to a world we glimpse only through the window of our train, as we hurry from one important city to another: a provincial world of dilapidated farmhouses and sagging apartment blocks, overgrown cemeteries and village drunks; a world seemingly abandoned by God — and yet full of the basic human joy of life itself.

Buy it > www.glagoslav.com

A BURGLAR OF THE BETTER SORT
by Tytus Czyżewski

The history of Poland, since the eighteenth century, has been marked by an almost unending struggle for survival. From 1795 through 1945, she was partitioned four times by her stronger neighbours, most of whom were intent on suppressing if not eradicating Polish culture. It is not surprising, then, that much of the great literature written in modern Poland has been politically and patriotically engaged. Yet there is a second current as well, that of authors devoted above all to the craft of literary expression, creating 'art for art's sake,' and not as a didactic national service. Such a poet is Tytus Czyżewski, one of the chief, and most interesting, literary figures of the twentieth century. Growing to maturity in the benign Austrian partition of Poland, and creating most of his works in the twenty-year window of authentic Polish independence stretching between the two world wars, Czyżewski is an avant-garde poet, dramatist and painter who popularised the new approach to poetry established in France by Guillaume Apollinaire, and was to exert a marked influence on such multi-faceted artists as Tadeusz Kantor.

Buy it > www.glagoslav.com

The Mouseiad and other Mock Epics
by Ignacy Krasicki

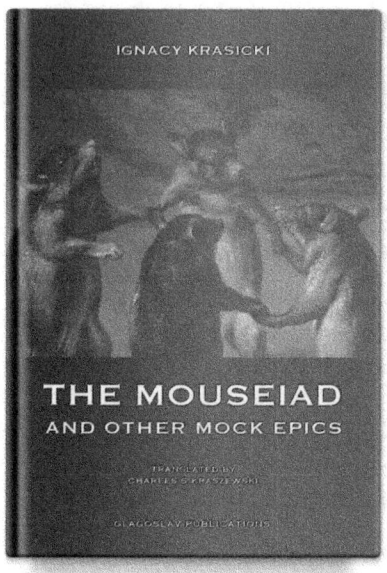

International brigades of mice and rats join forces to defend the rodents of Poland, threatened with extermination at the paws of cats favoured by the ancient ruler King Popiel, a sybaritic, cowardly ruler... The Hag of Discord incites a vicious rivalry between monastic orders, which only the good monks' common devotion to... fortified spirits... is able to allay... The present translation of the mock epics of Poland's greatest figure of the Enlightenment, Ignacy Krasicki, brings together the Mouseiad, the Monachomachia, and the Anti-monachomachia — a tongue-in-cheek 'retraction' of the former work by the author, criticised for so roundly (and effectively) satirising the faults of the Church, of which he himself was a prince. Krasicki towers over all forms of eighteenth-century literature in Poland like Voltaire, Swift, Pope, and LaFontaine all rolled into one. While his fables constitute his most well-known works of poetry, in the words of American comparatist Harold Segel, 'the good bishop's mock-epic poems [...] are the most impressive examples of his literary gifts.' This English translation by Charles S. Kraszewski is rounded off by one of Krasicki's lesser-known works, The Chocim War, the poet's only foray into the genre of the serious, Vergilian epic.

Buy it > www.glagoslav.com

The Sonnets
by Adam Mickiewicz

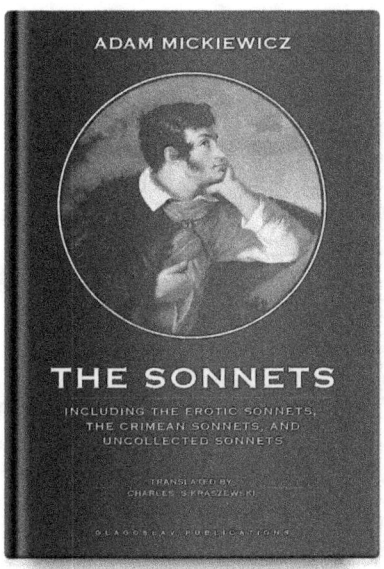

Because the poetry of Adam Mickiewicz is so closely identified with the history of the Polish nation, one often reads him as an institution, rather than a real person. In the *Crimean and Erotic Sonnets* of the national bard, we are presented with the fresh, real, and striking poetry of a living, breathing man of flesh and blood. Mickiewicz proved to be a master of Petrarchan form. His *Erotic Sonnets* chronicle the development of a love affair from its first stirrings to its disillusioning denouement, at times in a bitingly sardonic tone. *The Crimean Sonnets*, a verse account of his journeys through the beautiful Crimean Peninsula, constitute the most perfect cycle of descriptive sonnets since du Bellay. *The Sonnets* of Adam Mickiewicz are given in the original Polish, in facing-page format, with English verse translations by Charles S. Kraszewski. Along with the entirety of the Crimean and Erotic Sonnets, other "loose" sonnets by Mickiewicz are included, which provide the reader with the most comprehensive collection to date of Mickiewicz's sonneteering. Fronted with a critical introduction, *The Sonnets* of Adam Mickiewicz also contain generous textual notes by the poet and the translator.

Buy it > www.glagoslav.com

FOREFATHERS' EVE
by Adam Mickiewicz

Forefathers' Eve [*Dziady*] is a four-part dramatic work begun circa 1820 and completed in 1832 – with Part I published only after the poet's death, in 1860. The drama's title refers to *Dziady*, an ancient Slavic and Lithuanian feast commemorating the dead. This is the grand work of Polish literature, and it is one that elevates Mickiewicz to a position among the "great Europeans" such as Dante and Goethe.

With its Christian background of the Communion of the Saints, revenant spirits, and the interpenetration of the worlds of time and eternity, *Forefathers' Eve* speaks to men and women of all times and places. While it is a truly Polish work – Polish actors covet the role of Gustaw/Konrad in the same way that Anglophone actors covet that of Hamlet – it is one of the most universal works of literature written during the nineteenth century. It has been compared to Goethe's Faust – and rightfully so…

Buy it > www.glagoslav.com

Four Plays:
Mary Stuart, Kordian, Balladyna, Horsztyński

The dramas in Glagoslav's edition of *Four Plays* include some of the poet's greatest dramatic works, all written before age twenty-five: *Mary Stuart*, *Balladyna* and *Horsztyński* weave carefully crafted motifs from *King Lear*, *Macbeth*, *Hamlet* and *A Midsummer Night's Dream* in astoundingly original works, and *Kordian* — Słowacki's riposte to Mickiewicz's *Forefathers' Eve*, constitutes the final word in the revolutionary period of Polish Romanticism.

Translated into English by Charles S. Kraszewski, the *Four Plays* of Juliusz Słowacki will be of interest to aficionados of Polish Romanticism, Shakespeare, and theatre in general.

Buy it > www.glagoslav.com

www.ingramcontent.com/pod-product-compliance
Lightning Source LLC
Chambersburg PA
CBHW081338080526
44588CB00017B/2664